We Should All
Be Feminists

Also by Chimamanda Ngozi Adichie

Americanah
The Thing Around Your Neck
Half of a Yellow Sun
Purple Hibiscus

We Should All Be Feminists

Chimamanda Ngozi Adichie

ANCHOR BOOKS

A Division of Random House LLC • New York

AN ANCHOR BOOKS ORIGINAL, FEBRUARY 2015

Copyright © 2012, 2014 by Chimamanda Ngozi Adichie

We Should All Be Feminists was first presented as a TED Talk
given in the United Kingdom at TEDxEuston, in 2012.

ISBN: 978-1-101-91176-1
eBook ISBN: 978-1-101-8293-2

Cover design by Joan Wong

www. anchorbooks.com

Introduction

This is a modified version of a talk I delivered in December 2012 at TEDxEuston, a yearly conference focused on Africa. Speakers from diverse fields deliver concise talks aimed at challenging and inspiring Africans and friends of Africa. I had spoken at a different TED conference a few years before, giving a talk titled 'The Danger of the Single Story' about how stereotypes limit and shape our thinking, especially about Africa. It seems to me that the word *feminist*, and the idea of feminism itself, is also limited by stereotypes. When my

3

brother Chuks and best friend Ike, both co-organizers of the TEDxEuston conference, insisted that I speak, I could not say no. I decided to speak about feminism because it is something I feel strongly about. I suspected that it might not be a very popular subject, but I hoped to start a necessary conversation. And so that evening as I stood onstage, I felt as though I was in the presence of family – a kind and attentive audience, but one that might resist the subject of my talk. At the end, their standing ovation gave me hope.

We Should All Be Feminists

Okoloma was one of my greatest childhood friends. He lived on my street and looked after me like a big brother: if I liked a boy, I would ask Okoloma's opinion. Okoloma was funny and intelligent and wore cowboy boots that were pointy at the tips. In December 2005, in a plane crash in southern Nigeria, Okoloma died. It is still hard for me to put into words how I felt. Okoloma was a person I could argue with, laugh with and truly talk to. He was also the first person to call me a feminist.

I was about fourteen. We were in his house, arguing, both of us bristling with half-baked knowledge from the books we had read. I don't remember what this particular argument was about. But I remember that as I argued and argued, Okoloma looked at me and said, 'You know, you're a feminist.'

It was not a compliment. I could tell from his tone – the same tone with which a person would say, 'You're a supporter of terrorism.'

I did not know exactly what this word *feminist* meant. And I did not want Okoloma to know that I didn't know. So I brushed it aside and continued to argue. The first thing I planned to do when I got home was look up the word in the dictionary.

Now fast-forward to some years later.

In 2003, I wrote a novel called *Purple Hibiscus*, about a man who, among other things, beats his wife, and whose story doesn't end too well. While I was promoting the novel in Nigeria, a journalist, a nice, well-meaning man, told me he wanted to advise me. (Nigerians, as you might know, are very quick to give unsolicited *advice*.)

He told me that people were saying my novel was feminist, and his advice to me – he was shaking his head sadly as he spoke – was that I should never call myself a feminist, since feminists are women who are unhappy because they cannot find husbands.

So I decided to call myself a Happy Feminist.

Then an academic, a Nigerian woman, told me that feminism was not our culture, that feminism was un-African, and I was only calling myself a feminist because I had been influenced by Western books. (Which amused me, because much of my early reading was decidedly unfeminist: I must have read every single Mills & Boon romance published before I was sixteen. And each time I try to read those books called 'classic feminist texts', I get bored, and I struggle to finish them.)

Anyway, since feminism was un-African, I decided I would now call myself a Happy African Feminist. Then a dear friend told me that calling myself a feminist meant that I hated men. So I decided I would now be a Happy African Feminist Who Does Not Hate Men. At some point I was a Happy African Feminist Who Does Not Hate Men And Who Likes To Wear Lip Gloss And High Heels For Herself And Not For Men.

Of course much of this was tongue-in-cheek, but what it shows is how that word *feminist* is so heavy with baggage, negative baggage: you hate men, you hate bras, you hate African culture, you think women should always be in charge, you don't wear make-up, you don't shave, you're always angry, you don't have a sense of humour, you don't use deodorant.

Now here's a story from my childhood.

When I was in primary school in Nsukka, a university town in south-eastern Nigeria, my teacher said at the beginning of term that she would give the class a test and whoever got the highest score would be the class monitor. Class monitor was a big deal. If you were class monitor, you would write down the names of noise-makers each day, which was heady enough power on its own, but my teacher would also give you a cane to hold in your hand while you walked around and patrolled the class for noise-makers. Of course, you were not allowed to actually *use* the cane. But it was an exciting prospect for the nine-year-old me. I very much wanted to be class monitor. And I got the highest score on the test.

Then, to my surprise, my teacher said the monitor had to be a boy. She had forgotten to make that clear earlier; she assumed it was obvious. A boy had the second-highest score on the test. And *he* would be monitor.

What was even more interesting is that this boy was a sweet, gentle soul who had no interest in patrolling the class with a stick. While *I* was full of ambition to do so.

But I was female and he was male and he became class monitor.

I have never forgotten that incident.

If we do something over and over again, it becomes normal. If we see the same thing over and over again, it becomes normal. If only boys are made class monitor, then at some point we will all think, even if unconsciously, that the class monitor has to be a boy. If we keep seeing only men as heads of corporations, it starts to seem 'natural' that only men should be heads of corporations.

I often make the mistake of thinking that something that is obvious to me is just as obvious to everyone else. Take my dear friend Louis, who is a brilliant, progressive man. We would have conversations and he would tell me, 'I don't see what you mean by things being different and harder for women. Maybe it was so in the past, but not now. Everything is fine now for women.' I didn't understand how Louis could not see what seemed so evident.

I love being back home in Nigeria, and spend much of my time there in Lagos, the largest city and commercial hub of the country. Sometimes, in the evenings when the heat goes down and the city has a slower pace, I go out with friends and family to restaurants or cafés. On one of those evenings, Louis and I were out with friends.

There is a wonderful fixture in Lagos: a sprinkling of energetic young men who hang around outside certain establishments and very dramatically 'help' you park your car. Lagos is a metropolis of almost twenty million people, with more energy than London, more entrepreneurial spirit than New York, and so people come up with all sorts of ways to make a living. As in most big cities, finding parking in the evenings can be difficult, so these young men make a business out of finding spots and – even when there are spots available – of guiding you into yours with much gesticulating, and promising to 'look after' your car until you get back. I was impressed with the particular theatrics of the man who found us a parking spot that evening. And so as we were leaving, I decided to give him a tip. I opened my bag, put my hand inside my bag to get my money, and I gave it to the man. And he, this man who was happy and grateful, took the money from me, and then looked across at Louis and said, 'Thank you, sah!'

Louis looked at me, surprised, and asked, 'Why is he thanking me? I didn't give him the money.' Then I saw realization dawn on Louis's face. The man believed that whatever money I had ultimately came from Louis. Because Louis is a man.

Men and women are different. We have different hormones and different sexual organs and different biological abilities – women can have babies, men cannot. Men have more testosterone and are, in general, physically stronger than women. There are slightly more women than men in the world – 52 per cent of the world's population is female but most of the positions of power and prestige are occupied by men. The late Kenyan Nobel peace laureate Wangari Maathai put it simply and well when she said, 'The higher you go, the fewer women there are.'

In the recent US elections, we kept hearing of the Lilly Ledbetter law, and if we go beyond that nicely alliterative name, it was really about this: in the US, a man and a woman are doing the same job, with the same qualifications, and the man is paid more *because* he is a man.

So in a literal way, men rule the world. This made sense – a thousand years ago. Because human beings lived then in a world in which physical strength was the most important attribute for survival; the physically stronger person was more likely to lead. And men in general are physically stronger. (There are of course many exceptions.) Today, we live in a vastly different world. The person more qualified to lead is *not* the physically stronger person. It is the more intelligent, the more knowledgeable, the more creative, more innovative. And there are no hormones for those attributes. A man is as likely as a woman to be intelligent, innovative, creative. We have evolved. But our ideas of gender have not evolved very much.

Not long ago, I walked into the lobby of one of the best Nigerian hotels, and a guard at the entrance stopped me and asked me annoying questions – What was the name and room number of the person I was visiting? Did I know this person? Could I prove that I was a hotel guest by showing him my key card? – because the automatic assumption is that a Nigerian female walking into a hotel alone is a sex worker. Because a Nigerian female alone cannot possibly be a guest paying for her own room. A man who walks into the same hotel is not harassed. The assumption is that he is there for something legitimate. (Why, by the way, do those hotels not focus on the *demand* for sex workers instead of on the ostensible *supply*?)

In Lagos, I cannot go alone into many reputable clubs and bars. They just don't let you in if you are a woman *alone*. You must be accompanied by a man. And so I have male friends who arrive at clubs and end up going in with their arms linked with those of a complete stranger, because that complete stranger, a woman out on her own, had no choice but to ask for 'help' to get into the club.

Each time I walk into a Nigerian restaurant with a man, the waiter greets the man and ignores me. The waiters are products of a society that has taught them that men are more important than women, and I know that they don't intend harm, but it is one thing to know something intellectually and quite another to feel it emotionally. Each time they ignore me, I feel invisible. I feel upset. I want to tell them that I am just as human as the man, just as worthy of acknowledgement.

These are little things, but sometimes it is the little things that sting the most.

Not long ago, I wrote an article about being young and female in Lagos. And an acquaintance told me that it was an angry article, and I should not have made it so angry. But I was unapologetic. Of course it was angry. Gender as it functions today is a grave injustice. I am angry. We should all be angry. Anger has a long history of bringing about positive change. But I am also hopeful, because I believe deeply in the ability of human beings to remake themselves for the better.

But back to anger. I heard the caution in the acquaintance's tone, and I knew that the comment was as much about the article as it was about my character. Anger, the tone said, is particularly not good for a woman. If you are a woman, you are not supposed to express anger, because it is threatening. I have a friend, an American woman, who took over a managerial position from a man. Her predecessor had been considered a 'tough go-getter'; he was blunt and hard-charging and was particularly strict about the signing of time sheets. She took on her new job, and imagined herself equally tough, but perhaps a little kinder than him – he didn't always realize that people had families, she said, and she did. Only weeks into her new job, she disciplined an employee about a forgery on a time sheet, just as her predecessor would have done. The employee then complained to top management about her style. She was aggressive and difficult to work with, the employee said. Other employees agreed. One said they had expected that she would bring a 'woman's touch' to her job, but she hadn't.

It didn't occur to any of them that she was doing the same thing for which a man had been praised.

I have another friend, also an American woman, who has a high-paying job in advertising. She is one of two women in her team. Once, at a meeting, she said she had felt slighted by her boss, who had ignored her comments and then praised something similar when it came from a man. She wanted to speak up, to challenge her boss. But she didn't. Instead, after the meeting, she went to the bathroom and cried, then called me to vent about it. She didn't want to speak up because she didn't want to seem aggressive. She let her resentments simmer.

What struck me – with her and with many other female American friends I have – is how invested they are in being 'liked'. How they have been raised to believe that their being likeable is very important and that this 'likeable' trait is a specific thing. And that specific thing does not include showing anger or being aggressive or disagreeing too loudly.

We spend too much time teaching girls to worry about what boys think of them. But the reverse is not the case. We don't teach boys to care about being likeable. We spend too much time telling girls that they cannot be angry or aggressive or tough, which is bad enough, but then we turn around and either praise or excuse men for the same reasons. All over the world, there are so many magazine articles and books telling women what to do, how to be and not to be, in order to attract or please men. There are far fewer guides for men about pleasing women.

I teach a writing workshop in Lagos and one of the participants, a young woman, told me that a friend had told her not to listen to my 'feminist talk'; otherwise she would absorb ideas that would destroy her marriage. This is a threat – the destruction of a marriage, the possibility of not having a marriage at all – that in our society is much more likely to be used against a woman than against a man.

Gender matters everywhere in the world. And I would like today to ask that we should begin to dream about and plan for a different world. A fairer world. A world of happier men and happier women who are truer to themselves. And this is how to start: we must raise our daughters differently. We must also raise our sons differently.

We do a great disservice to boys in how we raise them. We stifle the humanity of boys. We define masculinity in a *very* narrow way. Masculinity is a hard, small cage, and we put boys inside this cage.

We teach boys to be afraid of fear, of weakness, of vulnerability. We teach them to mask their true selves, because they have to be, in Nigerian-speak, a *hard man*.

In secondary school, a boy and a girl go out, both of them teenagers with meagre pocket money. Yet the boy is expected to pay the bills, always, to prove his masculinity. (And we wonder why boys are more likely to steal money from their parents.)

What if both boys and girls were raised *not* to link masculinity and money? What if their attitude was not 'the boy has to pay', but rather, 'whoever has more should pay'?

Of course, because of their historical advantage, it is mostly men who *will* have more today. But if we start raising children differently, then in fifty years, in a hundred years, boys will no longer have the pressure of proving their masculinity by material means.

But by far the worst thing we do to males – by making them feel they have to be hard – is that we leave them with *very* fragile egos. The *harder* a man feels compelled to be, the weaker his ego is.

And then we do a much greater disservice to girls, because we raise them to cater to the fragile egos of males.

We teach girls to shrink themselves, to make themselves smaller.

We say to girls, 'You can have ambition, but not too much. You should aim to be successful but not too successful, otherwise you will threaten the man. If you are the breadwinner in your relationship with a man, pretend that you are not, especially in public, otherwise you will emasculate him.'

But what if we question the premise itself? Why should a woman's success be a threat to a man? What if we decide to simply dispose of that word – and I don't know if there is an English word I dislike more than this – *emasculation*.

A Nigerian acquaintance once asked me if I was worried that men would be intimidated by me.

I was not worried at all – it had not even occurred to me to be worried, because a man who would be intimidated by me is exactly the kind of man I would have no interest in.

Still, I was struck by this. Because I am female, I'm expected to aspire to marriage.

I am expected to make my life choices always keeping in mind that marriage is the most important. Marriage can be a good thing, a source of joy, love and mutual support. But why do we teach girls to aspire to marriage, yet we don't teach boys to do the same?

I know a Nigerian woman who decided to sell her house because she didn't want to intimidate a man who might want to marry her.

I know an unmarried woman in Nigeria who, when she goes to conferences, wears a wedding ring because she wants her colleagues to – according to her – 'give her respect'.

The sadness in this is that a wedding ring will indeed automatically make her seem worthy of respect, while not wearing a wedding ring would make her easily dismissible – and this is in a modern workplace.

I know young women who are under so much pressure – from family, from friends, even from work – to get married that they are pushed to make terrible choices.

Our society teaches a woman at a certain age who is unmarried to see it as a deep personal failure. While a man at a certain age who is unmarried has not quite come around to making his pick.

It is easy to say, 'But women can just say no to all this.' But the reality is more difficult, more complex. We are all social beings. We internalize ideas from our socialization.

Even the language we use illustrates this. The language of marriage is often a language of ownership, not a language of partnership.

We use the word *respect* for something a woman shows a man, but not often for something a man shows a woman.

Both men and women will say, 'I did it for peace in my marriage.'

When men say it, it is usually about something they should not be doing anyway. Something they say to their friends in a fondly exasperated way, something that ultimately proves to them their masculinity – 'Oh, my wife said I can't go to clubs every night, so now, for peace in my marriage, I go only on weekends.'

When women say 'I did it for peace in my marriage,' it is usually because they have given up a job, a career goal, a dream.

We teach females that in relationships, compromise is what a woman is more likely to do.

We raise girls to see each other as competitors – not for jobs or accomplishments, which in my opinion can be a good thing, but for the attention of men.

We teach girls that they cannot be sexual beings in the way boys are. If we have sons, we don't mind knowing about their girlfriends. But our daughters' boyfriends? God forbid. (But we of course expect them to bring home the perfect man for marriage when the time is right.)

We police girls. We praise girls for virginity but we don't praise boys for virginity (and it makes me wonder how exactly this is supposed to work out, since the loss of virginity is a process that usually involves two people of opposite genders).

Recently a young woman was gang-raped in a university in Nigeria, and the response of many young Nigerians, both male and female, was something like this: 'Yes, rape is wrong, but what is a girl doing in a room with four boys?'

Let us, if we can, forget the horrible inhumanity of that response. These Nigerians have been raised to think of women as inherently guilty. And they have been raised to expect so little of men that the idea of men as savage beings with no self-control is somehow acceptable.

We teach girls shame. *Close your legs. Cover yourself.* We make them feel as though by being born female, they are already guilty of something. And so girls grow up to be women who cannot say they have desire. Who silence themselves. Who cannot say what they truly think. Who have turned pretence into an art form.

I know a woman who hates domestic work, but she pretends that she likes it, because she has been taught that to be 'good wife material', she has to be – to use that Nigerian word – *homely*. And then she got married. And her husband's family began to complain that she had changed. Actually, she had not changed. She just got tired of pretending to be what she was not.

The problem with gender is that it prescribes how we *should* be rather than recognizing how we are. Imagine how much happier we would be, how much freer to be our true individual selves, if we didn't have the weight of gender expectations.

Boys and girls are undeniably different biologically, but socialization exaggerates the differences, and then starts a self-fulfilling process. Take cooking, for example. Today, women in general are more likely to do housework than men – cooking and cleaning. But why is that? Is it because women are born with a cooking gene or because over the years they have been socialized to see cooking as their role? I was going to say that perhaps women *are* born with a cooking gene until I remembered that the majority of famous cooks in the world – who are given the fancy title of 'chef' – are men.

I used to look at my grandmother, a brilliant woman, and wonder what she would have been if she'd had the same opportunities as men during her youth. Today, there are more opportunities for women than there were during my grandmother's time, because of changes in policy and law, which are very important.

But what matters even more is our attitude, our mindset.

What if, in raising children, we focus on *ability* instead of gender? What if we focus on *interest* instead of gender?

I know a family who has a son and a daughter, a year apart in age, both brilliant at school. When the boy is hungry, the parents say to the girl, 'Go and cook Indomie noodles for your brother.' The girl doesn't like to cook Indomie noodles, but she is a girl and she has to. What if the parents, from the beginning, taught *both* children to cook them? Cooking, by the way, is a useful and practical life skill for a boy to have. I've never thought it made much sense to leave such a crucial thing – the ability to nourish oneself – in the hands of others.

I know a woman who has the same degree and same job as her husband. When they get back from work, she does most of the house-work, which is true for many marriages, but what struck me was that whenever he changed the baby's nappy, she said *thank you* to him. What if she saw it as something normal and natural, that he should help care for his child?

I am trying to unlearn many lessons of gender I internalized while growing up. But I sometimes still feel vulnerable in the face of gender expectations.

The first time I taught a writing class in graduate school, I was worried. Not about the teaching material, because I was well prepared and I was teaching what I enjoyed. Instead I was worried about what to wear. I wanted to be taken seriously.

I knew that because I was female, I would automatically have to *prove* my worth. And I was worried that if I looked too feminine, I would not be taken seriously. I really wanted to wear my shiny lip gloss and my girly skirt, but I decided not to. I wore a very serious, very manly and very ugly suit.

The sad truth of the matter is that when it comes to appearance, we start off with men as the standard, as the norm. Many of us think that the less feminine a woman appears, the more likely she is to be taken seriously. A man going to a business meeting doesn't wonder about being taken seriously based on what he is wearing – but a woman does.

I wish I had not worn that ugly suit that day. Had I then the confidence I have now to be myself, my students would have benefited even more from my teaching. Because I would have been more comfortable and more fully and truly myself.

I have chosen to no longer be apologetic for my femininity. And I want to be respected in all my femaleness. Because I deserve to be. I like politics and history and am happiest when having a good argument about ideas. I am girly. I am happily girly. I like high heels

and trying on lipsticks. It's nice to be co
mented by both men and women (altho
have to be honest and say that I prefer
compliments of stylish women), but I often
wear clothes that men don't like or don't
'understand'. I wear them because I like them
and because I feel good in them. The 'male
gaze', as a shaper of my life's choices, is
largely incidental.

Gender is not an easy conversation to have.
It makes people uncomfortable, sometimes
even irritable. Both men and women
are resistant to talk about gender, or are
quick to dismiss the problems of gender.
Because thinking of changing the status quo
is always uncomfortable.

Some people ask, 'Why the word *feminist*? Why not just say you are a believer in human rights, or something like that?' Because that would be dishonest. Feminism is, of course, part of human rights in general – but to choose to use the vague expression *human rights* is to deny the specific and particular problem of gender. It would be a way of pretending that it was not women who have, for centuries, been excluded. It would be a way of denying that the problem of gender targets women. That the problem was not about being human, but specifically about being a female human. For centuries, the world divided human beings into two groups and then proceeded to exclude and oppress one group. It is only fair that the solution to the problem should acknowledge that.

Some men feel threatened by the idea of feminism. This comes, I think, from the insecurity triggered by how boys are brought up, how their sense of self-worth is diminished if *they* are not 'naturally' in charge as men.

Other men might respond by saying, 'Okay, this is interesting, but I don't think like that. I don't even think about gender.'

Maybe not.

And that is part of the problem. That many men do not actively *think* about gender or notice gender. That many men say, like my friend Louis did, that things might have been bad in the past but everything is fine now. And that many men do nothing to change it. If you are a man and you walk into a restaurant and the waiter greets just you, does it occur to you to ask the waiter, 'Why have you not greeted her?' Men need to speak out in all of these ostensibly small situations.

Because gender can be uncomfortable, there are easy ways to close this conversation.

Some people will bring up evolutionary biology and apes, how female apes bow to male apes – that sort of thing. But the point is this: we are not apes. Apes also live in trees and eat earthworms. We do not.

Some people will say, 'Well, poor men also have a hard time.' And they do.

But that is not what this conversation is about. Gender and class are different. Poor men still have the privileges of being men, even if they do not have the privileges of being wealthy. I learned a lot about systems of oppression and how they can be blind to one another by talking to black men. I was once talking about gender and a man said to me, 'Why does it have to be you as a woman? Why not you as a human being?' This type of question is a way of silencing a person's specific experiences. Of course I am a human being, but there are particular things that happen to me in the world because I am a woman. This same man, by the way, would often talk about his experience as a black man. (To which I should probably have responded, 'Why not your experiences as a man or as a human being? Why a black man?')

So, no, this conversation is about gender. Some people will say, 'Oh, but women have the real power: bottom power.' (This is a Nigerian expression for a woman who uses her sexuality to get things from men.) But bottom power is not power at all, because the woman with bottom power is actually not powerful; she just has a good route to tap another person's power. And then what happens if the man is in a bad mood or sick or temporarily impotent?

Some people will say a woman is subordinate to men because it's our culture. But culture is constantly changing. I have beautiful twin nieces who are fifteen. If they had been born a hundred years ago, they would have been taken away and killed. Because a hundred years ago, Igbo culture considered the birth of twins to be an evil omen. Today that practice is unimaginable to all Igbo people.

What is the point of culture? Culture functions ultimately to ensure the preservation and continuity of a people. In my family,

I am the child who is most interested in the story of who we are, in ancestral lands, in our tradition. My brothers are not as interested as I am. But I cannot participate, because Igbo culture privileges men, and only the male members of the extended family can attend the meetings where major family decisions are taken. So although I am the one who is most interested in these things, I cannot attend the meeting. I cannot have a formal say. Because I am female.

Culture does not make people. People make culture. If it is true that the full humanity of women is not our culture, then we can and must make it our culture.

I think very often of my friend Okoloma. May he and others who passed away in that Sosoliso crash continue to rest in peace. He will always be remembered by those of us who loved him. And he was right, that day, many years ago, when he called me a feminist. I am a feminist.

And when, all those years ago, I looked the word up in the dictionary, it said: *Feminist: a person who believes in the social, political and economic equality of the sexes.*

My great-grandmother, from stories I've heard, was a feminist. She ran away from the house of the man she did not want to marry and married the man of her choice. She refused, protested, spoke up whenever she felt she was being deprived of land and access because she was female. She did not know that word *feminist*. But it doesn't mean she

47

wasn't one. More of us should reclaim that word. The best feminist I know is my brother Kene, who is also a kind, good-looking and very masculine young man. My own definition of a feminist is a man or a woman who says, 'Yes, there's a problem with gender as it is today and we must fix it, we must do better.'

All of us, women and men, must do better.

About the Author

Chimamanda Ngozi Adichie grew up in Nigeria. Her work has been translated into thirty languages and has appeared in various publications, including *The New Yorker*, *Granta*, *The O. Henry Prize Stories*, the *Financial Times*, and *Zoetrope: All-Story*. She is the author of the novels *Purple Hibiscus*, which won the Commonwealth Writers' Prize and the Hurston/Wright Legacy Award; *Half of a Yellow Sun*, which won the Orange Prize and was a National Book Critics Circle Award Finalist, a *New York Times* Notable

Book, and a *People* and *Black Issues Book Review* Best Book of the Year; and *Americanah*, which won the National Book Critics Circle Award and was a *New York Times*, *Washington Post*, *Chicago Tribune*, and *Entertainment Weekly* Best Book of the Year; and the story collection *The Thing Around Your Neck*. A recipient of a MacArthur Fellowship, she divides her time between the United States and Nigeria.

www.chimamanda.com
www.facebook.com/chimamandaadichie

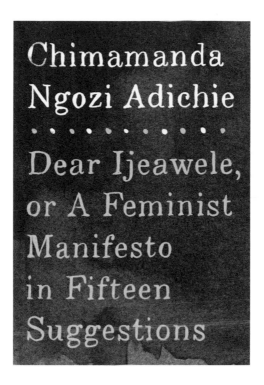

Chimamanda
Ngozi Adichie

· · · · · · · · · ·

Dear Ijeawele,
or A Feminist
Manifesto
in Fifteen
Suggestions

From the best-selling author of *Americanah*
and *We Should All Be Feminists* comes a powerful
new statement about feminism today…written
as a letter from one friend to another.

 KNOPF

Available in hardcover and eBook from Knopf